D1352458

PSALMS

of patience, protest and praise

Twenty-four new psalm settings by
John L Bell

Wild Goose Publications
The Iona Community
Glasgow

© The Iona Community 1993
ISBN 0 947988 56 4

Published by Wild Goose Publications
The Iona Community
Pearce Institute
840 Govan Road
Glasgow G51 3UU

Cover designed by Blue Peach, Glasgow
Music origination by Jeanne Fisher, Ludlow, Shropshire
Printed in Great Britain by The Cromwell Press, Melksham, Wiltshire

Contents

Introduction

One of the greatest slurs on the 150 Old Testament poems known collectively and affectionately as The Psalms is to call them 'praise songs'. This not only shows a frightening blindness to the content of the poems, it also belittles the experience of Jesus Christ. When, on the cross, he used the words 'My God, my God, why have you forsaken me?' was he singing a happy chorus?

The reason for the abiding place of The Psalms in Christian worship, both public and private, is that they cover in theme and expression, the whole gamut of human experience. Exhuberance, delight and unbridled joy are there. So also are questioning, curiosity and impatience. So also are agony, loneliness and deep despair.

This range of human condition is what The Psalms seek to offer God, not for approval but so that the relationship between the people of God and their maker might be honest at all times. In this era of history, when the ending of the Cold War and global awareness of international disorders have not ensured that the world is safer or less hungry, or its wealthy inhabitants more fulfilled, it may be that we have to learn to use these ancient words in ways that will ensure our present-day apprehensions and pains are offered to God as earnestly as our most exhuberant praise.

The psalm settings in this collection are not of one sort. The Wild Goose Worship Group, with whom I have collaborated in their writing, has repeatedly confronted me with the inadequacy of one formula – be that common metre, Anglican chant or Catholic antiphon – to express the sometimes pensive, sometimes dialogical nature of the original words and their intention. Additionally, respect has had to be paid to whether the settings would best suit solo singing (many of the psalms are of a highly personal nature) and whether or not they should be sung with accompaniment.

With regard to the words, I have tried to ensure that the language is gender-inclusive. However, the issue of the gendering of God has not been as easy to deal with. In Britain (as among some black communities in the USA) there is no ban on 'Lord', especially when the word is seen as the exclusive property of God. When it comes to personal pronouns, 'he' is very occasionally used, though (as in Psalm 131) the feminine within God, which is explicit in The Psalms, is recognised. At the end of the day, all language for or about God is metaphorical. What I have aimed to do here is to walk in advance of the debate within Scotland, while at the same time refusing to treat God as less than a person for the sake of political correctness.

In the preparation of this collection, no small indebtedness must be recorded to the writing of Artur Weiser (*The Psalms*, SCM 1962) and Bernard Anderson (*Out of the Depths*, Westminster Press 1983). Their exegesis and insights regarding the nature and purpose of The Psalms have been of immense value in seeking for a translation, paraphrase or metricization that would both respect the integrity of the original poems and communicate with freshness to contemporary worshippers.

Beyond these, I must express a personal appreciation to two of my seniors. It was during the ministry of Revd A Cameron Gibson in Fenwick, Ayrshire, that my love for the metrical psalmody of my own tradition was engendered, and it is to him that I owe my incessant fascination for the potential of unaccompanied congregational singing. My deep gratitude is also due to the Very Revd Professor Robert Davidson, whose passion for the language and literature of the Psalms, and of the Old Testament at large, has both infected and affected my faith, writing and outlook. To both of these this book is fondly dedicated.

JOHN L BELL
JUNE 1993

Fondly dedicated to
A Cameron Gibson
and
Robert Davidson

Happy is the one

Ps. 1

Tune: Benedictus Primus (JLB)

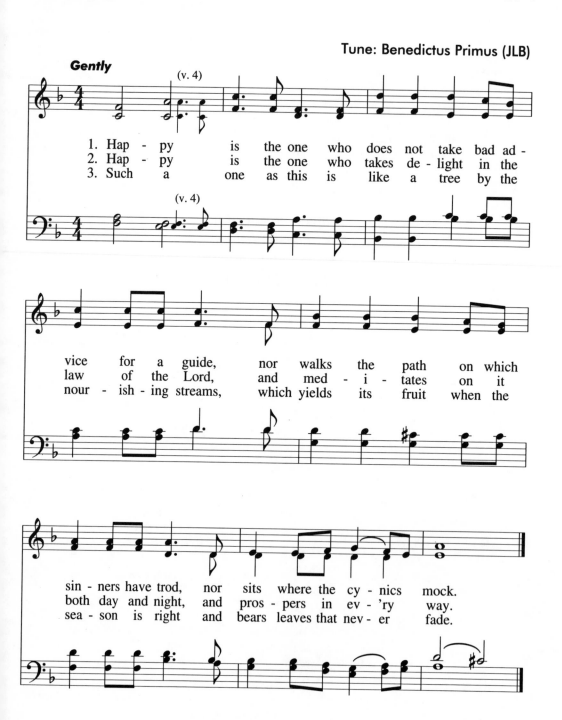

Gently (v. 4)

1. Hap - py is the one who does not take bad ad -
2. Hap - py is the one who takes de - light in the
3. Such a one as this is like a tree by the

vice for a guide, nor walks the path on which
law of the Lord, and med - i - tates on it
nour - ish - ing streams, which yields its fruit when the

sin - ners have trod, nor sits where the cy - nics mock.
both day and night, and pros - pers in ev - 'ry way.
sea - son is right and bears leaves that nev - er fade.

1. Happy is the one
    who does not take bad advice for a guide,
    nor walks the path on which sinners have trod,
    nor sits where the cynics mock.

2. Happy is the one
    who takes delight in the law of the Lord,
    and meditates on it both day and night,
    and prospers in every way.

3. Such a one as this
    is like a tree by the nourishing streams,
    which yields its fruit when the season is right
    and bears leaves that never fade.

(Optional verses)
4. Not so the wicked's fate;
    for they, like chaff which the wind blows away,
    will never stand and be confident
    on God's great judgement day.

5. Nor will sinners walk
    among the assembly of God's own folk;
    for wicked ways are all doomed by the Lord
    who blesses the honest path.

This wisdom song with which the Book of Psalms begins is in the style of the beatitudes we find in Luke's Gospel. There Jesus indicates both who is blessed and who is cursed. For most purposes – as an introit or congregational song – the first three verses would be sufficient. However, if the psalm were the basis of preaching or meditation, all verses should be employed. It should be sung confidently but gently, as an affirmation rather than a boast.

Hear me, Lord, and draw near Ps. 6

Tune: Troubled Soul (JLB)

Slowly and steadily

1. Hear me Lord, and draw near; in
2. Lord, how long will you tar - ry? Come
3. I am worn out with grief: ev - 'ry
4. Lord, you hear how I cry; the

mer - cy, lis - ten to my plea: I am worn
quick - ly, come to my dis - tress; in
night con - fu - sion fills my mind, my
sound of weep - ing fills your ears. I

out, wea - ry and ex - haust - ed, and my
kind - ness, res - cue me from death, let me
pil - low is soaked with tears and my
trust in you for de - liv - 'rance and an

soul	is	trou - bled deep with - in	me.	
see	the	day when I can praise	you.	
eyes	are	dim and sore with weep -	ing.	
end	to	all that now de - feats	me.	

1. Héar me, Lórd, and draw néar;
   in mércy, lísten to my pléa:
   I am worn óut, wéary and exháusted,
   and my sóul is tróubled deep withín me.

2. Lórd, how lóng will you tárry?
   Come quíckly, cóme to my distréss;
   in kíndness, réscue me from déath,
   let me sée the dáy when I can práise you.

3. Í am worn óut with gríef:
   every níght confúsion fills my mínd,
   my píllow is sóaked with téars
   and my éyes are dím and sore with wéeping.

4. Lórd, you héar how I crý;
   the sóund of wéeping fills your éars.
   I trúst in yóu for delíverance
   and an énd to áll that now deféats me.

Psalm 6, here paraphrased, is an individual psalm of lament in which the worshipper pours out anxiety, frustration and mental anguish before God. In order to allow the force of the words to be felt, the verses are not in strict metre, but are rather set as a chant, thereby enabling the natural speech rhythms to be replicated in song. This item might best be sung by a choir to ensure precision in phrasing.

O Lord, our Lord

Ps. 8

Tune: Tramps and Hawkers (Scottish Trad.)

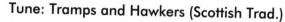

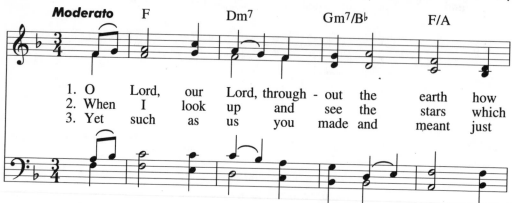

1. O Lord, our Lord, through - out the earth how
2. When I look up and see the stars which
3. Yet such as us you made and meant just

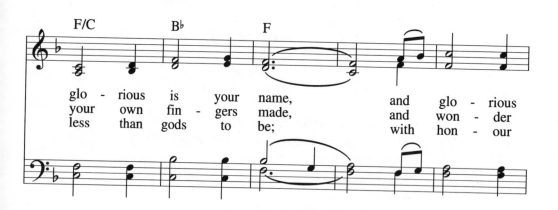

glo - rious is your name, and glo - rious
your own fin - gers made, and won - der
less than gods to be; with hon - our

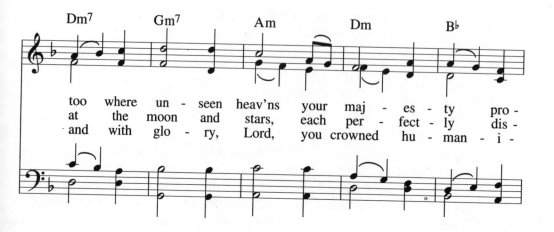

too where un - seen heav'ns your maj - es - ty pro -
at the moon and stars, each per - fect - ly dis -
and with glo - ry, Lord, you crowned hu - man - i -

claim. On in - fant lips, in chil - dren's song a
played; then must I ask, 'Why do you care? Why
ty. And then do - min - ion you be - stowed for

strong de - fence you raise to coun - ter e - ne -
love hu - man - i - ty? And why keep ev - 'ry
all made by your hand, all sheep and cat - tle,

my and threat, and foil the re - bel's ways.
mor - tal name fixed in your mem - o - ry?'
birds and fish that move through sea or land.

CODA

O Lord, our Lord, through - out the earth how

9

glo - rious is your name!

1. O Lord, our Lord, throughout the earth
   how glorious is your name,
   and glorious too where unseen heavens
   your majesty proclaim.
   On infant lips, in children's song
   a strong defence you raise
   to counter enemy and threat,
   and foil the rebel's ways.

2. When I look up, and see the stars
   which your own fingers made,
   and wonder at the moon and stars,
   each perfectly displayed;
   then must I ask, 'Why do you care?
   Why love humanity?
   And why keep every mortal name
   fixed in your memory?'

3. Yet such as us you made and meant
   just less than gods to be;
   with honour and with glory, Lord,
   you crowned humanity.
   And then dominion you bestowed
   for all made by your hand,
   all sheep and cattle, birds and fish
   that move through sea or land.

   CODA
   O Lord, our Lord, throughout the earth
   how glorious is your name!

Psalm 8 is a song of praise which ponders the beauty of creation not as an end in itself but as the arena in which we see the bounty and kindness of God. It is one of the psalms which Jesus alluded to, towards the end of his life. His critics were annoyed at the sound of children in the temple singing his praises, and he compounded their uneasiness by suggesting that they were doing what God had ordained.

This metricization is in double common metre. It could be sung to a common metre tune, in which case the number of verses would be doubled and the coda would have to be omitted or replaced by a repetition of verse 1. Here it is set to a tune associated with travelling folk in Scotland, whose presence has at times been as much an irritant to the genteel as the sound of children was to the Pharisees.

May the words of my mouth   Ps. 19

Tune: Seearem (JLB)

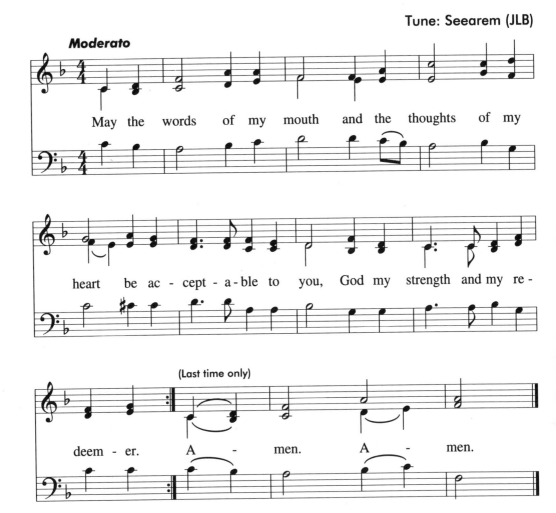

May the words of my mouth
and the thoughts of my heart
be acceptable to you,
God my strength and my redeemer.
(Amen. Amen.)

Psalm 19 ends with this short prayer. Frequently the same words are used by preachers before a sermon and may well be employed by all worshippers at the beginning of a service. If required, the words may be changed from the singular to the plural. The Amen is optional.

My shepherd is the Lord

Ps. 23

Tune: Bonnyton (JLB)

1. My shep - herd is the Lord my God; no good thing shall I need. In green - est fields he'll let me lie, to rest - ful streams he'll lead.
2. The Lord re - vives the soul in me, and for his own name's sake, he guides me and en - sures my feet the prop - er path - ways take.
3. Should I through deep - est dark - ness walk, no e - vil need I fear; for you are with me, you whose staff and crook mean strength is near.
4. And look, in my op - pres - sor's sight, a ta - ble you have spread; you fill my cup to o - ver - flow, and oil an - noints my head.
5. Good - ness and love which nev - er fail shall all my life at - tend, and in the house of God the Lord my years, with joy, I'll spend.

1. My shepherd is the Lord my God;
   no good thing shall I need.
   In greenest fields he'll let me lie,
   to restful streams he'll lead.

2. The Lord revives the soul in me,
   and for his own name's sake,
   he guides me and ensures my feet
   the proper pathways take.

3. Should I through deepest darkness walk,
   no evil need I fear;
   for you are with me, you whose staff
   and crook mean strength is near.

4. And look, in my oppressor's sight,
   a table you have spread;
   you fill my cup to overflow,
   and oil annoints my head.

5. Goodness and love which never fail
   shall all my life attend,
   and in the house of God the Lord
   my years, with joy, I'll spend.

The image of God as Shepherd has amazingly deep resonances, even in urban society. It was, for example, the preferred depiction of Christ that workers in the Glasgow City Mission identified from conversations with prostitutes meeting in their refuges. Sadly, this psalm is often relegated to sentimental use at funerals, though that was never its original intention.

It is actually a great psalm of Christ's passion, prefiguring to some extent the events of Holy Week, and its resonances come to life when used in the season of Lent.

I lift my soul to you, O God

Ps. 25

Tune: Tender Care (JLB)

Confidently

1. I lift my soul to you, O God. In you I
2. No - one who ev - er trusts in you shall find their
3. Make known your paths to me, O Lord; show me the
4. Re - mem - ber Lord, your ten - der care, your nev - er

trust, in you a - lone. Save me from
hope is put to shame. Shame comes to
ways which I should take. Teach me and
fail - ing, con - stant love. For - give my

shame and from de - feat lest my op -
those who turn a - way, who spurn the
lead me, faith - ful God; you are my
sins, my youth's of - fence; in love and

Words & Music © 1993 The Iona Community / Wild Goose Publications, Glasgow, UK

po - nents	should	gloat	o - ver	me.
good - ness	of the	liv -	ing	God.
sa - viour	and my	hope	is in	you.
kind - ness	re -	mem - ber	me	Lord.

1. I lift my soul to you, O God.
   In you I trust, in you alone.
   Save me from shame and from defeat
   lest my opponents should gloat over me.

2. No-one whoever trusts in you
   shall find their hope is put to shame.
   Shame comes to those who turn away,
   who spurn the goodness of the living God.

3. Make known your paths to me, O Lord;
   show me the ways which I should take.
   Teach me and lead me, faithful God;
   you are my saviour and my hope is in you.

4. Remember, Lord, your tender care,
   your never failing, constant love.
   Forgive my sins, my youth's offence;
   in love and kindness remember me, Lord.

While Psalm 25 ends on a note of lament and entreaty, its first seven verses, here paraphrased, speak of trust and assurance. There is deep yet direct honesty in these words as in all the psalms relating to personal experience. For that reason, it may best be sung solo with the congregation giving their listening to the worship as the singer offers the song.

In you, O Lord, I found refuge   Ps. 31

Tune: Farrellette (JLB)

Confidently

ANTIPHON   Em   Am⁷   D   Gmaj⁷   C   Am   Bm⁷   Em

In you, O Lord, I found ref-uge; let me nev-ermore be put to shame.

VERSE   A⁷   Am⁷/G   Fmaj⁷

1. By your sav - ing pow'r de - liv - er me,
2. Be a rock of ref - uge to save me, be a
3. Set me free from the net spread to catch me; for
4. Faith - ful God, your grace has saved me; in

   Bm   Bm⁷/A   Gmaj⁷

bend down your ear and hear me; come
strong for - tress to shield me; Lord
you, O Lord, are my safe - ty; in -
love you saw my af - flic - tion and

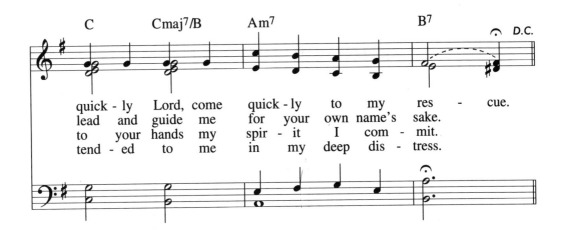

quick - ly Lord, come quick - ly to my res - cue.
lead and guide me for your own name's sake.
to your hands my spir - it I com - mit.
tend - ed to me in my deep dis - tress.

ANTIPHON

In you, O Lord, I found refuge;
let me nevermore be put to shame.

VERSE

1. By your sáving pówer delíver me,
   bénd down your éar and héar me;
   come qúickly Lórd, come
   qúickly tó my réscue.

2. Be a róck of réfuge to sáve me,
   be a stróng fórtress to shíeld me;
   Lord léad and gúide me
   fór your ówn name's sáke.

3. Set me frée from the nét spread to cátch me
   for yóu, O Lórd, are my sáfety;
   intó your hánds my
   spírit Í commít.

4. Faithful Gód, your gráce has sáved me;
   in lóve you sáw my afflíction
   and ténded tó me
   ín my déep distréss.

Verses 1–4 and 7 of Psalm 31 are here sung in a style particularly favoured by the Roman Catholic Church. A chorus or antiphon is sung once by a soloist, then repeated by the congregation. Thereafter the soloist sings the verses, at the end of which the congregation sings in response. It is a very helpful way of allowing the psalm to be sung with understanding and integrity.

I waited patiently for God

Ps. 40

Tune: Amazing Grace (Scottish trad.)

1. I waited patiently for God, for God to hear my pray'r; and God bent down to where I sank and listened to me there.

2. God raised me from a miry pit, from mud and sinking sand, and set my feet upon a rock where I can firmly stand.

3. And on my lips a song was put, a new song to the Lord. Many will marvel open-eyed and put their trust in God.

(Hum)

4. Great won – ders you have done, O Lord, all pur – posed for our good. Un – a – ble ev – 'ry one to name, I bow in grat – i – tude.

1. I waited patiently for God,
   for God to hear my prayer;
   and God bent down to where I sank
   and listened to me there.

2. God raised me from a miry pit,
   from mud and sinking sand,
   and set my feet upon a rock
   where I can firmly stand.

3. And on my lips a song was put,
   a new song to the Lord.
   Many will marvel, open-eyed
   and put their trust in God.

4. Great wonders you have done, O Lord,
   all purposed for our good.
   Unable every one to name,
   I bow in gratitude.

This metricization in common metre of Psalm 40.1–5 is aptly wedded to the tune popularly known as 'Amazing Grace'. The sentiment of the psalm is that of gratitude, but it has a profundity about it, rather than a superficial thankfulness.

For the best singing of this psalm, let verse 1 be solo; verse 2 solo with hummed accompaniment; verse 3 a canon at the bar, and verse 4 in four-part harmony. There should be no difficulty in getting a congregation that knows the tune to sing in canon, as long as it is clear which sector comes in when. A conductor or precentor is therefore required.

This particular version of the song may not be familiar to everyone. Throughout Britain and the USA, the triplets in the melody are included, replaced or omitted according to the geographical area. Similarly, the last syllable of line two in each verse may have two rather than five beats. Please feel free to amend as suits.

Just as a lost and thirsty deer   Ps. 42

Tune: Thirsting for God (JLB)

Lamentoso

1. Just as a lost and thirs - ty deer
2. Both day and night I cry a - loud;
3. Bro - ken and hurt, I call to mind
4. Why am I now so lost and low?

longs for a cool and run - ning stream,
tears have be - come my on - ly food,
how in the past I served the Lord,
why am I trou - bl'd and con - fused?

I thirst for you, the liv - ing God,
while all a - round cruel voi - ces ask,
wor - shipped and walked with hap - py crowds
Giv - en no an - swer, still I hope

anx - ious to know that you are near.
'Where is your God? Where is your God?'
sing - ing and shout - ing praise to God.
and trust my Sav - iour and my God.

1. Just as a lost and thirsty deer
   longs for a cool and running stream,
   I thirst for you, the living God,
   anxious to know that you are near.

2. Both day and night I cry aloud;
   tears have become my only food,
   while all around cruel voices ask,
   'Where is your God? Where is your God?'

3. Broken and hurt, I call to mind
   how in the past I served the Lord,
   worshipped and walked with happy crowds
   singing and shouting praise to God.

4. Why am I now so lost and low?
   Why am I troubled and confused?
   Given no answer, still I hope
   and trust my Saviour and my God.

Psalm 42 is a very poignant lament of someone for whom the days of fulfilling faith and worship seem in the past. Fate, choice or circumstance has removed the individual from his or her own spiritual roots and the memory of the happy past contrasts with a depressing present.

This paraphrase of vv 1–5 is in long metre. When using this tune, it is very evocative to have the middle two verses sung solo with the other voices humming their parts.

Clap your hands all you nations Ps. 47

Tune: Marius (JLB)

Brightly

1. Clap your hands all you na - tions,
2. God sub - dues ev - 'ry na - tion,
3. To the shout - ing in tri - umph, *A - men. Hal - le - lu - jah!*
4. Praise the Lord with your sing - ing,
5. Those on earth who are migh - ty

shout for joy all you peo - ple;
God is king of all crea - tures;
to the blast - ing of trum - pets, *A - men. Hal - le - lu - jah!*
sing God psalms for ev - er.
still be - long to our Ma - ker,

Ho - ly is the most high;
God has giv - en this land
God has gone up, *A - men. Hal - le - lu - jah!*
God is mon - arch of all,
God ex - alt - ed on high

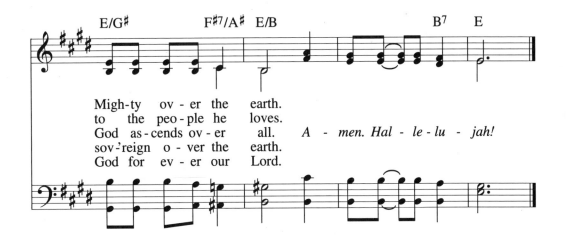

Migh-ty ov - er the earth.
to the peo - ple he loves.
God as - cends ov - er all. A - men. Hal - le - lu - jah!
sov-'reign o - ver the earth.
God for ev - er our Lord.

1. Clap your hands all you nations,
   Amen. Hallelujah!
   shout for joy all you people;
   Amen. Hallelujah!
   Holy is the most high;
   Amen. Hallelujah!
   mighty over the earth.
   Amen. Hallelujah!

2. God subdues every nation,
   God is king of all creatures;
   God has given this land
   to the people he loves.

3. To the shouting in triumph,
   to the blasting of trumpets,
   God has gone up,
   God ascends over all.

4. Praise the Lord with your singing,
   sing God psalms for ever.
   God is monarch of all,
   sovereign over the earth.

5. Those on earth who are mighty
   still belong to our Maker,
   God exalted on high,
   God forever our Lord.

According to Artur Weiser, this psalm might have been used to commemorate a specific historical high point; or it may have been intended to look to the fulfilment of God's kingdom; or it may have been a liturgical song used to celebrate the enthronement of God in the midst of the worship of the people. Or it could have elements of all three.

Whatever the case, it is a song of great celebration and demands a lively tune which should motivate the feet as much as the mouth. Percussion and other instruments can be freely used with this setting, as can dance. If required, it can be sung antiphonally, with a group singing the words of the verse and the congregation responding with *Amen. Hallelujah!*

Let the giving of thanks

Ps. 50

Tune: Greyfriars (JLB)

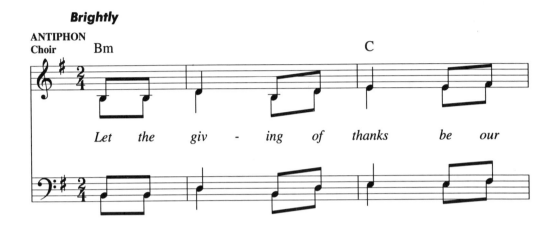

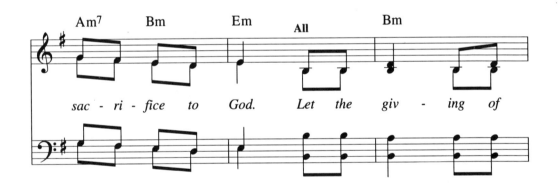

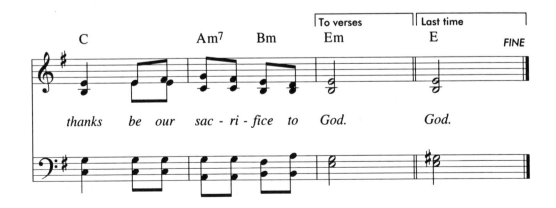

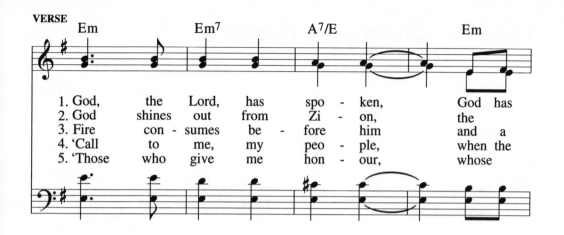

1. God, the Lord, has spo - ken, God has
2. God shines out from Zi - on, the
3. Fire con - sumes be - fore him and a
4. 'Call to me, my peo - ple, when the
5. 'Those who give me hon - our, whose

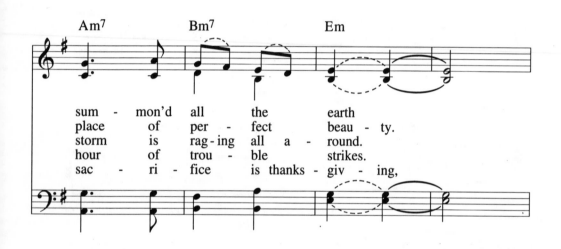

sum - mon'd all the earth
place of per - fect beau - ty.
storm is rag - ing all a - round.
hour of trou - ble strikes.
sac - ri - fice is thanks - giv - ing,

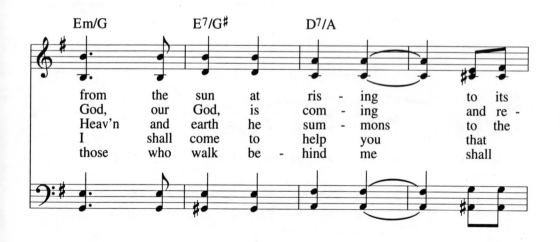

from the sun at ris - ing to its
God, our God, is com - ing and re -
Heav'n and earth he sum - mons to the
I shall come to help you that
those who walk be - hind me shall

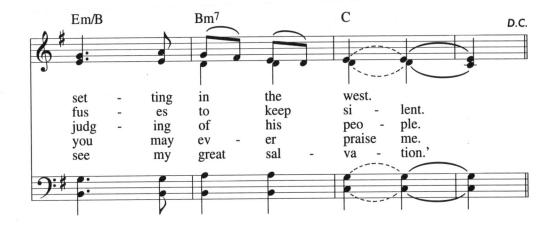

set - ting in the west.
fus - es to keep si - lent.
judg - ing of his peo - ple.
you may ev - er praise me.
see my great sal - va - tion.'

ANTIPHON
Let the giving of thanks
be our sacrifice to God.

1. God, the Lord, has spoken
   God has summoned all the earth
   from the sun at rising
   to its setting in the west.

2. God shines out from Zion,
   the place of perfect beauty.
   God, our God, is coming
   and refuses to keep silent.

3. Fire consumes before him
   and a storm is raging all around.
   Heaven and earth he summons
   to the judging of his people.

4. 'Call to me, my people,
   when the hour of trouble strikes.
   I shall come to help you
   that you may ever praise me.

5. 'Those who give me honour,
   whose sacrifice is thanksgiving,
   those who walk behind me
   shall see my great salvation.'

Psalm 50 is much longer than the five verses offered here. It is a liturgical song which celebrates how God is not bribed by predictable sacrifices, but rather is praised by worship which comes from a grateful heart. The antiphon is found in verse 14 of the psalm, and the rest of the text is from vv 1–4, 15 & 23.

Depending on the musical culture of the congregation, some people may find the first six notes a simple but unusual combination. There may be a temptation to sing D♯ rather than D♮. People who regularly sing minor, modal or pentatonic melodies will not have this difficulty.

In my day of fear

Ps. 56

Tune: Distant Oaks (JLB)

ANTIPHON

In my day of fear, I put my trust in you, God most high.

VERSE

1. All day long I am un - der at - tack, my
2. In God's word I have put my faith, in
3. All day long they wound me with words, and
4. But you, O Lord, you have no - ted my grief and
5. I will de - clare with due grat - i - tude how

en - e - mies are al - ways near; ly - ing in wait,
you I trust, O Lord, most high. There-fore I need no
ev - 'ry word is meant to harm; band - ing to - geth - er,
seen my end - less mis - er - y; keep all my tears
God has kept my soul from death; thus in God's pres - ence

| G7 | | C | Am7 | F#m7 | B7 | D.C. |

wait - ing their chance, in - tend - ing to har - rass and fight.
long - er fear, for what could mor - tals ev - er do?
plot - ting their worst, they sly - ly watch my ev - 'ry move.
stored in your flask, the tears re - cord - ed in your book.
I glad - ly walk, in pres - ence of the light of life.

ANTIPHON
In my day of fear
I put my trust in you,
God most high.

1. All day long I am under attack,
   my enemies are always near;
   lying in wait, waiting their chance
   intending to harass and fight.

2. In God's word I have put my faith,
   in you I trust, O Lord, most high.
   Therefore I need no longer fear,
   for what could mortals ever do?

3. All day long they wound me with words,
   and every word is meant to harm;
   banding together, plotting their worst,
   they slyly watch my every move.

4. But you, O Lord, you have noted my grief
   and seen my endless misery;
   keep all my tears stored in your flask,
   the tears recorded in your book.

5. I will declare with due gratitude
   how God has kept my soul from death;
   thus in God's presence I gladly walk,
   in presence of the light of life.

Malicious gossip, slander and lying tongues are all proscribed in scripture. And that happens not just in the Psalms. It is a theme which runs through the Prophets, the Gospels and the New Testament letters.

People in every age are 'wounded with words'. This psalm, a portion of which (vv 1–6, 8, & 12–13) is offered here, may speak to and for their situation.

For its best effect, the antiphon should be sung twice at the commencement. The first time, a soloist introduces the antiphon, then the congregation repeats it. Thereafter it is sung once at the conclusion of each verse.

On God alone I wait silently   Ps. 62

Tune: Strong Tower (JLB)

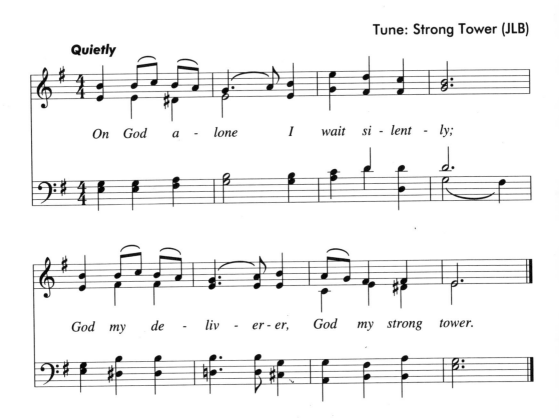

On God a - lone I wait si - lent - ly;

God my de - liv - er - er, God my strong tower.

On God alone I wait silently;
God my deliverer, God my strong tower.

The Psalms are full of phrases which are worth pondering on their own. This text is contracted from the first two verses of Psalm 62 and may be sung repeatedly as a meditation, or as a song preparatory to worship. Or it can be used as a congregational response during prayers.

When using it, have a solo voice sing the tune once, followed by the whole company singing together.

O God, you are my God alone Ps. 63

Tune: Resignation (Trad.)

Gently

1. O God, you are my God a-
2. Your faith - ful love sur - pass - es
3. Through - out the night I lie in

lone, whom ea - ger - ly I seek, though
life, e - vok - ing all my praise. Through
bed and call you, Lord, to mind; in

long - ing fills my soul with thirst and leaves my
ev - 'ry day, to bless your name, my hands in
dark - est hours I med - i - tate how God, my

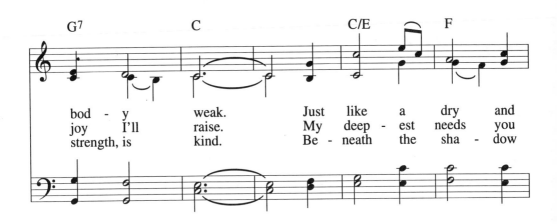

bod - y weak. Just like a dry and
joy I'll raise. My deep - est needs you
strength, is kind. Be - neath the sha - dow

bar - ren land a - waits a fresh - 'ning show'r,
sat - is - fy as with a sump - tuous feast.
of your wing, I live and feel se - cure;

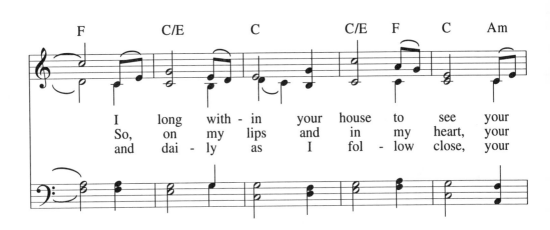

I long with - in your house to see your
So, on my lips and in my heart, your
and dai - ly as I fol - low close, your

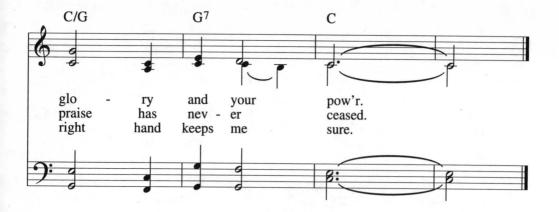

| C/G | G7 | C |

glo - ry and your pow'r.
praise has nev - er ceased.
right hand keeps me sure.

1. O God, you are my God alone,
   whom eagerly I seek,
   though longing fills my soul with thirst
   and leaves my body weak.
   Just like a dry and barren land
   awaits a freshening shower,
   I long within your house to see
   your glory and your power.

2. Your faithful love surpasses life,
   evoking all my praise.
   Through every day, to bless your name,
   my hands in joy I'll raise.
   My deepest needs you satisfy
   as with a sumptuous feast.
   So, on my lips and in my heart,
   your praise has never ceased.

3. Throughout the night I lie in bed
   and call you, Lord, to mind;
   in darkest hours I meditate
   how God, my strength, is kind.
   Beneath the shadow of your wing,
   I live and feel secure;
   and daily, as I follow close,
   your right hand keeps me sure.

This paraphrase of the first eight verses of Psalm 63 has a rare and intimate tenderness about the words. It is a song of personal trust and gratitude to God which is here complemented by a very lovely melody.

The origins of 'Resignation', as it is known in North America, are uncertain. It does not sound like an early American hymn tune, but rather may be a direct transplant or a derivative of a Scottish or Irish melody. A Gaelic precentor on the island of Skye said, on hearing this tune, that the sound of it moved him very deeply, somehow striking a chord in him of faith, culture and heritage.

O God, with holy righteousness — Ps. 72

Tune: Old 107th

With vigour

1. O God, with ho - ly right - eous - ness
2. Rul - ers and kings of for - eign lands
3. Long may his name last like the sun,

en - dow your roy - al son,
shall bow be - fore his throne,
long be his fame ex - press'd

that he may help your suff - 'ring folk
and all the na - tions of the world
as na - tions for like bless - ing pray

Words & Arrangement © 1993 The Iona Community / Wild Goose Publications, Glasgow, UK

and see your jus - tice done.
- shall make his will their own.
who see him as God's bless'd.

Through all the earth, from shore to shore,
For he shall res - cue those in need,
And bless'd be God, for God a - lone

his king - dom shall ex - tend;
pro - tect the fright - en'd poor
brings wond - rous things to birth;

his en - e - mies shall lick the dust,
and, in the face of ev - 'ry threat,
for ev - er let God's name be prais'd,

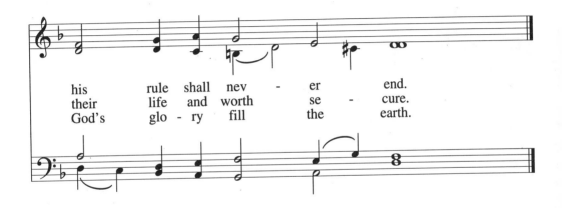

his   rule shall nev - er   end.
their   life and worth se - cure.
God's   glo - ry fill the earth.

1. O God, with holy righteousness
   endow your royal son,
   that he may help your suffering folk
   and see your justice done.
   Through all the earth, from shore to shore,
   his kingdom shall extend;
   his enemies shall lick the dust,
   his rule shall never end.

2. Rulers and kings of foreign lands
   shall bow before his throne,
   and all the nations of the world
   shall make his will their own.
   For he shall rescue those in need,
   protect the frightened poor
   and, in the face of every threat
   their life and worth secure.

3. Long may his name last like the sun,
   long be his fame expressed
   as nations for like blessing pray
   who see him as God's blessed.
   And blessed be God, for God alone
   brings wondrous things to birth;
   for ever let God's name be praised,
   God's glory fill the earth.

Psalm 72 is presumed to have been written for the enthronement of a king, possibly Solomon. It is a prayer of intercession for the king that he might match up to his task, not as a figurehead, but as an agent of God's justice. For this reason, the psalm is associated with the birth of Christ who fulfils and transforms expectations of divine monarchy. The above portion extracts vv 1, 2, 8–14 & 17–19.

The tune 'Old 107th' or 'Psalm 107' was either composed or arranged by Louis Bourgeois for the French Psalter of 1543. It is sometimes sung in a very stately fashion, but if (and it is a possibility) it has folk-tune origins, it might better be expressed with a lively tempo. It is in double common metre so there are plenty of alternatives.

Do not keep silent, O God

Ps. 83

Tune: Tempest Wind (JLB)

ANTIPHON

Do not keep silent, O God;
Be neither silent nor still.

VERSE

1. Your énemies ríse up in túmult,
   and thóse who háte you hóld their heads hígh.

2. They devíse a cunning plót against your péople,
   and conspíre against thóse whom you hóld so déar.

3. 'Let us wípe them out,' they sáy, 'as a nátion.
   Let the ónes God has chósen be knówn no móre.'

4. Scátter them, Lórd, like thístledown,
   like cháff which is blówn far awáy by the wínd.

5. Like a fíre ráging through the fórest
   pursúe your oppónents with your témpest wínd.

6. Then lét it be knówn, O Lórd,
   you alóne are Most Hígh over áll the éarth.

We have already found individual psalms of lament in this selection. Here we have a community lament – a protest song in which the people of God ask that those who are not merely political enemies but the enemies of heaven might be put down.

Such a sentiment may seem alien to us today. Perhaps, as Christians, we are reluctant to talk about enemies. If so, a look at the extremes of poverty and excess in the world, both attributable to human greed and selfishness, reminds us that enemies need not wear military uniforms, but may take the guise of money-lending agencies, multinational, ethic-free companies, or dictatorships of the left and right.

Since this is a community lament, the verses should be sung by several people – for example, men and women alternating. The last chord of the verse is intended to be discordant.

Whoever lives beside the Lord Ps. 91

Tune: Teann a nall (Scottish Trad.)

Calmly

1. Who - ev - er lives be - side the Lord,
2. From un - seen dan - ger and dis - ease
3. You will not dread what dark - ness brings —
4. A thou - sand may die at your side,
5. God says, 'I'll save from ev - 'ry harm

shelt - 'ring in th'Al - migh - ty's shade, shall
God will keep you safe and sure; be -
hid - den dan - ger, dead - ly plague; nor
thou - sands more fall close at hand; but
those who know and love my name. In

say, 'My God, in you I trust, my
neath his wings a place you'll find, a
will you fear, in day - light hours, the
with God's truth for strength and shield, no
trou - ble I will hon - our them and

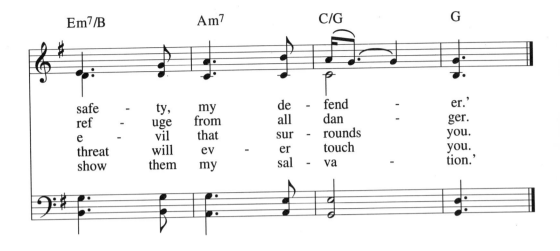

safe	-	ty,	my		de	-	fend	-		er.'
ref	-	uge	from		all		dan	-		ger.
e	-	vil	that		sur	-	rounds			you.
threat		will	ev	-	er		touch			you.
show		them	my		sal	-	va	-		tion.'

1. Whoever lives beside the Lord,
   sheltering in the Almighty's shade,
   shall say, 'My God, in you I trust,
   my safety, my defender.'

2. From unseen danger and disease
   God will keep you safe and sure;
   beneath his wings a place you'll find,
   a refuge from all danger.

3. You will not dread what darkness brings –
   hidden danger, deadly plague;
   nor will you fear in daylight hours,
   the evil that surrounds you.

4. A thousand may die at your side,
   thousands more fall close at hand;
   but with God's truth for strength and shield,
   no threat will ever touch you.

5. God says, 'I'll save from every harm
   those who know and love my name.
   In trouble I will honour them
   and show them my salvation.'

Psalm 91 and Romans 8 share the same sentiment: faith and hope in the face of danger and possible death. It is a song of trust which does not deny the realities of illness and other human torments, but undergirds them with a deep belief in the providence of God. Here vv 1-7 and 14-17 are metricized.

The tune is a beautiful Gaelic air from the island of South Uist in the Hebrides, harmonized a little unconventionally to ensure it sounds like a folk tune and not a hymn tune.

Praise your Maker

Ps. 117

Tune: Kort (JLB)

Praise your Ma - ker, all you na - tions;

and ex - tol him, all you peo - ple.

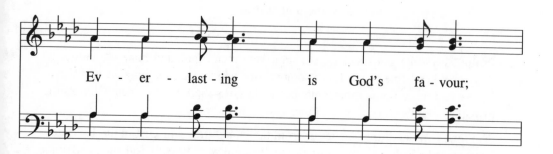

Ev - er - last - ing is God's fa - vour;

strong and con - stant love sur - rounds us.

Praise the Lord! Praise the Lord! A - men!

Praise the Lord! Al - le lu - ia! A - men! A - men!

Praise your Maker, all you nations;
and extol him, all you people.
Everlasting is God's favour;
strong and constant love surrounds us.

Praise the Lord!
Alleluia! Amen!

Psalm 117, the shortest in the book, is reckoned to be a call to worship, originally announced by the priest, inviting people to join together in celebration at a festival event.

It is therefore well suited to being sung as an introit by a choir, preferably at the rear of a church building where the suddenness and shortness of the piece can be a fitting call to corporate worship.

Lifting my eyes up to the hills   Ps. 121

Tune: Fecundity (JLB)

Moderato

(Solo) 1. Lift - ing my eyes up to the hills, where can I look for
2. The Lord who guards you nev - er sleeps, nor will he let you
3. God is your guard - ian, God your shade, pro - tec - tor of your
4. The Lord shall shield you from all harm and safe - ly guard your

aid? (All) Your help comes on - ly from the Lord who earth and
fall; no slum - ber drow - ses Is - rael's God, guard - ian of
right. By day the sun shall hurt you none, nor shall the
soul. For - ev - er, as you come and go, God's love shall

1.2.3. **D.C.** **Last time only**

hea - ven made.
each and all.
moon by night.

(4.) keep you whole.

SOLO

1. *Lifting my eyes up to the hills,*
   where can I look for aid?

   ALL
   Your help comes only from the Lord
   who earth and heaven made.

2. The Lord who guards you never sleeps,
   nor will he let you fall;
   no slumber drowses Israel's God,
   guardian of each and all.

3. God is your guardian, God your shade,
   protector of your right.
   By day the sun shall hurt you none,
   nor shall the moon by night.

4. The Lord shall shield you from all harm
   and safely guard your soul.
   Forever, as you come and go,
   God's love shall keep you whole.

Since 1650, Psalm 121 has been sung to the tune 'French' (first published in 1615) in a metricization which begins 'I to the hills will lift mine eyes. From whence doth come mine aid?' Despite the punctuation, the melodic line and the sound of the words have suggested that help comes from the hills. It is hoped that in this setting, the sentiment is clearer.

The psalm is, in fact, a pilgrim song in which the traveller, looking around and perhaps, like the Good Samaritan, being aware of danger lurking in the hills, asks where help comes from. The rest of the psalm provides the answer.

To express its original intention, it is good to have the first two lines of verse 1 sung solo, with the harmony parts hummed underneath. Then all join from line 3.

Out of the direst depths

Ps. 130

Tune: Southwell (1579)

Slowly

1. Out of the dir - est depths I
2. If you kept note of sins, be
4. Yes, with the Lord is grace and

make my deep - est plea. O gra - cious - ly bow
fore you who could stand? But since for - give - ness
pow'r to free and save. Re - demp - tion from their

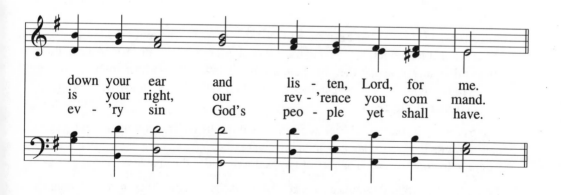

down your ear and lis - ten, Lord, for me.
is your right, our rev - 'rence you com - mand.
ev - 'ry sin God's peo - ple yet shall have.

1. Out of the direst depths
   I make my deepest plea.
   O graciously bow down your ear
   and listen, Lord, for me.

2. If you kept note of sins,
   before you who could stand?
   But since forgiveness is your right,
   our reverence you command.

3. My soul longs for the Lord,
   and hopes to hear God's word.
   More keenly than some watch for dawn,
   I wait and watch for God.

4. Yes, with the Lord is grace
   and power to free and save.
   Redemption from their every sin
   God's people yet shall have.

This was Martin Luther's favourite psalm and has long been revered in the Church as an expression of penitence and of God's deliverance.

The tune, 'Southwell', has been around since 1579 and has a beautiful and plaintive short metre melody. Here the original and an alternative harmonization are provided.

The pride from my heart

Ps. 131

Tune: The Isle of Mull (Scottish trad.)

Tenderly

1. For you the pride from my heart is ban - ish'd, for you false
2. Now is my soul calm from all its test - ing, like a wean'd

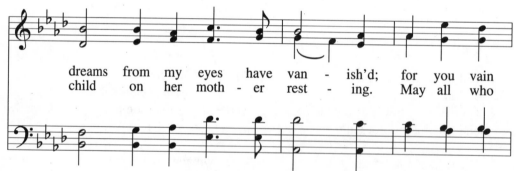

dreams from my eyes have van - ish'd; for you vain
child on her moth - er rest - ing. May all who

glo - ry I leave ad - mir - ing, end - less am -
hear join such cel - e - brat - ing; wait for the

bi - tion   I   cease   de - sir - ing.
Lord.   God   is   worth   our   wait - ing.

1. For you the pride from my heart is banished,
   for you false dreams from my eyes have vanished;
   for you vain glory I leave admiring,
   endless ambition I cease desiring.

2. Now is my soul calm from all its testing,
   like a weaned child on her mother resting.
   May all who hear join such celebrating;
   wait for the Lord. God is worth our waiting.

For many people, Psalm 131 is a stumbling block. How could we say or sing together in public words such as 'O Lord, my heart is not haughty, my eyes are not raised too high'? There seems to be an immodesty about the sentiment, a spiritual boasting.

Not so. The words were never intended to be shouted from the rooftops. They are words of intimate personal honesty, the kind of honesty which two lovers share after a quarrel, when one admits that he or she has been wrong, has been big-headed or has overestimated his or her capabilities. Then, forgiven and warmed by the love of the other, tranquillity is found.

The gentle Gaelic air known commonly as 'The Isle of Mull' expresses the warmth and love implicit in this psalm.

Beside the streams of Babylon   Ps. 137

Tune: Dunlap's Creek (Scottish Trad.)

Gently

1. Be - side the streams of Bab - y - lon, we
2. On wil - low trees we hung our harps while,
3. How shall we ev - er sing God's song in
4. And let my tongue stick in my mouth if

sat our - selves and wept, re - mem - ber - ing the
add - ing to their wrongs, our cap - tors smirk'd a
such a for - eign land? If I my birth - place
ev - er I for - get Je - ru - sa - lem, which

land we loved and all the hope it kept.
cruel re - quest, 'Sing, one of Zi - on's songs.'
dared for - get, let strength de - sert my hand.
far a - bove all oth - er joys I set.

1. Beside the streams of Babylon
   we sat ourselves and wept,
   remembering the land we loved
   and all the hope it kept.

2. On willow trees we hung our harps
   while, adding to their wrongs,
   our captors smirked a cruel request,
   'Sing, one of Zion's songs.'

3. How shall we ever sing God's song
   in such a foreign land?
   If I my birthplace dared forget,
   let strength desert my hand.

4. And let my tongue stick in my mouth
   if ever I forget
   Jerusalem, which far above
   all other joys I set.

As with Psalm 131, many people find it difficult to conceive how Psalm 137 might be used in public worship. It is the song of exiled people whose captors torment and taunt them. It ends with the curse, 'Happy is the one who takes your children and dashes them against a rock'.

A clue to its possible use may come from history. When, in the 18th century, absentee landlords required Scottish highland hills to be cleared of people in order that they might be populated with sheep, those dispossessed of their land were sometimes herded into boats and sent to North America. When they arrived there, in exile, having little to comfort them, they took solace in previously unsung psalms such as this. Legend has it that 'Dunlap's Creek' was the tune to which they sang the words.

It may therefore be as intercession for other exiles that we sing this psalm, not offering to God how we feel, but, for a moment, taking on our lips words which express the brokenness of refugees and exiles world-wide.

The final verse is omitted in this metricization, because its seemingly outrageous curse is better dealt with in preaching or group conversation. It should not be forgotten, especially by those who have never known exile, dispossession or the rape of people and land.

Sing to God with joy

Ps. 147

Tune: Glendon (JLB)

Sing to God, with joy and glad - ness,

hymns and psalms of grat - i - tude; with the voice of

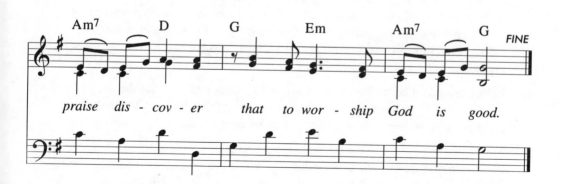

praise dis - cov - er that to wor - ship God is good.

VERSE

1. God u-nites his scat-ter'd peo-ple,
2. Such is God's great pow'r and wis-dom
3. God, with clouds, the sky has cur-tain'd,
4. God's dis-cern-ment nev-er fa-vours

gath-ers those who wan-der'd far,
none can cal-cu-late or tell;
thus en-sur-ing rain shall fall;
strength or speed to lift or move;

heals the hurt and bro-ken spir-its,
keen is God to ground the wick-ed
earth, re-spond-ing, grows to or-der
God de-lights in those who fear him,

tend-ing ev-'ry wound and scar.
and with hum-ble folk to dwell.
food for crea-tures great and small.
trust-ing in his stead-fast love.

D.C.

ANTIPHON

Sing to God, with joy and gladness,
hymns and psalms of gratitude;
with the voice of praise discover
that to worship God is good.

1. God unites his scattered people,
   gathers those who wandered far,
   heals the hurt and broken spirits,
   tending every wound and scar.

2. Such is God's great power and wisdom
   none can calculate or tell;
   keen is God to ground the wicked
   and with humble folk to dwell.

3. God, with clouds, the sky has curtained,
   thus ensuring rain shall fall;
   earth, responding, grows to order
   food for creatures great and small.

4. God's discernment never favours
   strength or speed to lift or move;
   God delights in those who fear him,
   trusting in his steadfast love.

The last six psalms in the Bible are songs of praise, reflecting different aspects of God's providence and love. Psalm 147, of which the first eleven verses are here paraphrased, deals with the graciousness of God in caring for exiled and broken people, as well as the generosity of God in providing sustenance for the earth.

As with other antiphonal psalms, a solo voice should sing the antiphon once, immediately followed by the congregation. Thereafter the choir or music group sings the verses.

Glory to God above!

Ps. 148

Tune: Wellington Hall (JLB)

With spirit

1. Glo - ry to God   a - bove!   Heav - ens de - clare
2. Glo - ry to God   be - low   let depths of o -
3. 'Glo - ry to God!'   now sing   com - mon - er, queen

La   la   la   la la   la   la   etc.

his   love;   praise him, you an - gels,   praise him all you
cean show;   light - ning and hail, snow   wind and cloud per -
and king;   wo - men and men of   ev - 'ry age u -

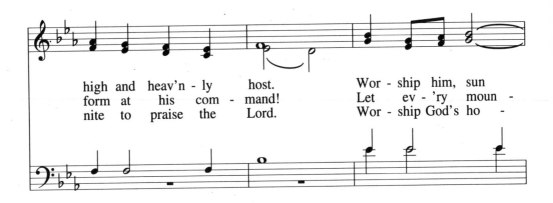

high and heav'n - ly   host.   Wor - ship him, sun
form at his com - mand!   Let ev - 'ry moun -
nite to praise the Lord.   Wor - ship God's ho -

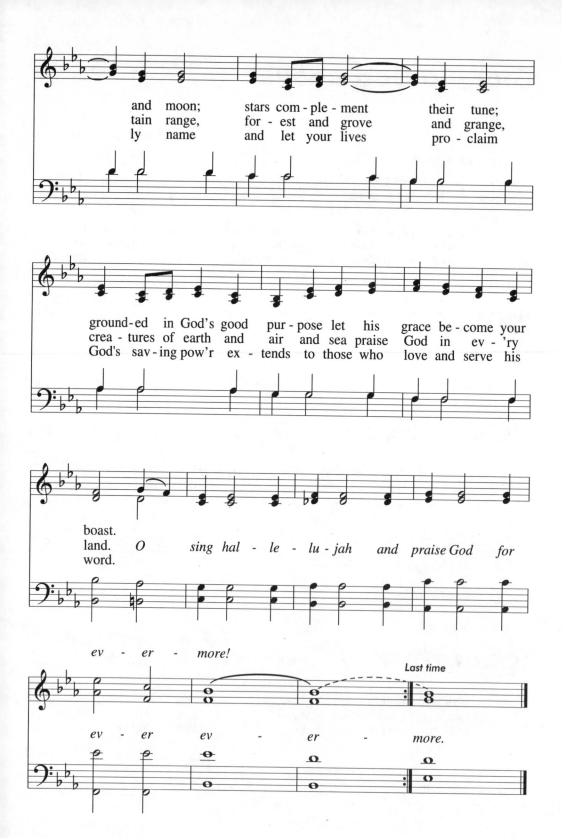

and moon;   stars com - ple - ment   their tune;
tain range,   for - est and grove   and grange,
ly name   and let your lives   pro - claim

ground-ed in God's good   pur - pose let his   grace be - come your
crea - tures of earth and   air and sea praise God in ev - 'ry
God's sav - ing pow'r ex - tends to those who love and serve his

boast.
land.   O   sing hal - le - lu - jah   and praise God for
word.

ev - er - more!

Last time

ev - er   ev - er - more.

1. Glory to God above!
   Heavens declare his love;
   praise him, you angels,
   praise him all you high and heavenly host.
   Worship him, sun and moon;
   stars, complement their tune;
   grounded in God's good purpose
   let his grace become your boast.
       O sing hallelujah
       and praise God for evermore!

2. Glory to God below
   let depths of ocean show;
   lightning and hail, snow
   wind and cloud perform at his command!
   Let every mountain range,
   forest and grove and grange,
   creatures of earth and air and sea
   praise God in every land.

3. 'Glory to God!' now sing
   commoner, queen and king;
   women and men of every age
   unite to praise the Lord.
   Worship God's holy name
   and let your lives proclaim
   God's saving power extends to those
   who love and serve his word.

Psalm 148 is a magnificent example of how the people of God have an ecological responsibility.

The psalm identifies three orders of creation engaged in the praise of God – the heavenly beings, the earth, and humanity. It is the middle order which we often exclude from being part of God's praise. Yet the Bible resonates with language about hills skipping, valleys laughing, seas roaring.

God has made the natural world to offer its praise. Humanity, charged with the stewardship of the earth, opposes the divine will if, through pollution, irradiation, deforestation or some other human negligence or design, the earth is prevented from offering its song.

In this setting, the three orders of creation are represented in different verses and, yes, the last chord does have a D natural!

Index of psalms

Index of tunes